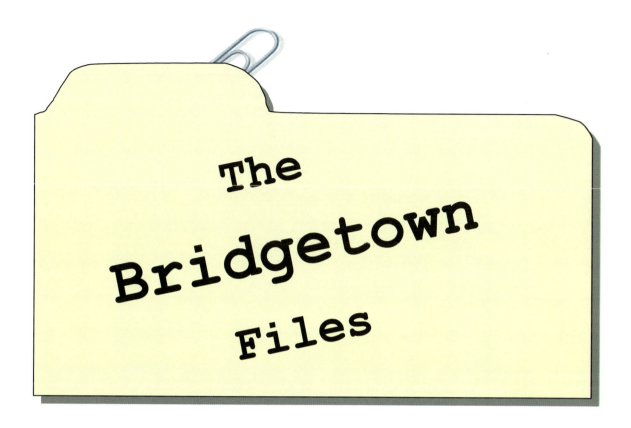

Developed and Created as a Homeschool Project by:

Forest B. Flynn   Elan M. Hess
Ann M. Hess

Copyright © 2014 Ann M. Hess

Created and Edited as a
Home School Project
by The Hess and Flynn Families
Illustrations by Elan Hess
Cover photo courtesy Rick Kellam

First Edition

ISBN-13: 978-1499146769
ISBN-10: 1499146760

All rights reserved.
Printed in the United States of America.
No part of this publication may be reproduced in any form or by any means, electronic, mechanical, photocopying, recording, or otherwise without prior permission of the authors.

Email: studios@feathertree3.com

This book is dedicated to the people who are curious.

ABOUT THIS BOOK

In the Fall of 2013, we started an "Eastern Shore" home school class with our son, Elan Hess and our neighbors, Forest and Liam Flynn. We interviewed people, read books, visited local places of interest, and did extensive research. It soon became clear that by focusing on our "own backyard" in Bridgetown, we could learn about American history, geography, cartography, science, architecture, deductive reasoning, computer skills, and who makes the best chocolate chip cookies!

Bridgetown dates to the 1600's and played a significant role in U.S. history. This book is a collection of some of the fascinating information that was shared with us. It is just the tip of the iceberg of what could be published! We hope it will inspire the reader to look more closely at Bridgetown and to become passionate about the history in their own backyard — wherever that is!

— Annie Hess, Co-learner and Project Advisor

May 2014

TABLE OF CONTENTS

File Name	Page Number
Dot Robbins' Essay	2
The Bridge of Bridgetown	11
Bridgetown in the E.S. News	18
Bridgetown Post Office	23
Hungars Church	26
Shorter's Chapel	29
Sam's Corner	31
Chatham	33
Winona	35
Grapeland	39
G. Fred Floyd	42
Pear Plain	44
Fun Facts	46
A Word of Thanks	53
Recommended Reading	53
About the Authors	54

~ Dot Robbins ~
Bridgetown Essay
1938

This award-winning essay is an excellent introduction to the history and significance of Bridgetown. Re-produced here with no changes to the original typed version done by Jane Dunton Turner. This essay was written thirteen years before Ralph Whitelaw wrote and published "Virginia's Eastern Shore."

> Dorothy "Dot" Robbins
>
> Valedictorian
>
> FRANKTOWN-NASSAWADOX
> HIGH SCHOOL
>
> Seniors graduated
> at 17 years of age
>
> The picture on the essay is
> not clear. My mother,
> Louise Floyd Dunton, 1st cousin to "Dot",
> had this picture which was taken
> in Ocean City, MD when "Dot"
> and Mama Louise went there.
> They were very close and grew up
> Together being best friends and
> like sisters.
>
> I, Jane Floyd Dunton Turner,
> retyped this essay in August of 2003
> making it more legible.
> I hope you enjoy reading this grand
> essay on Bridgetown done by my cousin
> and treasure it as much
> as I do.

This cover sheet of the essay, provides background on Dot Robbins and her family ties to Jane Floyd Dunton Turner. Jane is a dedicated genealogist, advocate for the importance of Native American heritage, and an excellent resource on life in Bridgetown. We are grateful to Jane for allowing us to make this wonderful essay available and for all of the information she shared with us!

THE NORTHAMPTON TIMES, CAPE CHARLES VIRGINIA

Old Home Prize Winning Essay by Franktown-Nassawadox Senior

"History of Bridgetown and Vicinity" by Dorothy Robbins

- - - - - - - - - - -

Whenever an Eastern Shoreman goes forth into other places of the world, he is likely to be greeted with some such phrase as "so you live on the good old Eastern Shore." Immediately this individual swells with pride, nods assents, and begins to talk about the Eastern Shore, for the most part, about the place in which he lives. But, truthfully, he doesn't know enough about his home town to talk to a stranger longer than thirty minutes.

If this citizen lives in the community around Bridgetown (Hungar's Creek) there are many interesting things he may be able to tell.

To begin with, Bridgetown, which is on the main bayside road leading down the Peninsula, is one of the few oldest towns on Del-Mar-Va, as the Eastern Shore is sometimes spoken of. Bridgetown was originally named Nusawattocks from the Indian tribe which inhabited that section. Nusawattocks means "a stream between two streams," and naturally because the body of water at Bridgetown is the small stream between the two large streams, the Chesapeake Bay and the Atlantic Ocean, the town was named Nusawattocks.

In 1524, Giovanna de Verrazano, an Italian, discovered the Eastern Shore, on which peninsula he found people living. In 1607 and 1608, Captain John Smith again explored this territory. He found Indians on the shore and these Indians called the entire territory "Ye Kingdom of Accawmacke." Six years after Smith's explorations the colonists began to immigrate to different places on the Eastern Shore. On June 14, 1614 Lieutenant Cradock and seventeen men were sent to the Eastern Shore to make salt for the colony at Jamestown. They settled at Dale's Gift on Old Plantation Creek.

In 1620, Secretary John Pory was granted 500 acres of land on King's Creek which became known as the "Secretary's Lands" and also as "Town Fields." That same year Pory laid out his lands and sent over his first tenants.

In 1621, which is as far back as the records about Bridgetown or Hungar's Creek date, King Debedeavon, chief of a tribe of Indians on the Shore, gave to Sir George Yeardley, Governor of the Virginia Colony, all the land between Hungar's Creek and Cheriton Creek. Sir George himself went over to Accawamacke to inspect his properties and he was very much pleased with what he found. In the census of 1624-5 there were 44 males, 7 females, 19 houses, 16 storehouses and one fort on the Eastern Shore. After 1626 land patents were issued in great numbers and settlements grew rapidly.

In the very earliest times, court was held at various places, namely the homes of private citizens according to the conveyances of the Justices and the lawyers. In 1632 a Monthly Court was established at Accomack. Court was carried on for a while in this manner. But when the right of trial by jury was instituted, the cabin in which the Accomack Court was held would not hold all the people. So from this time on Point House or Dinner House at "Old Plantation" became the lower county seat and Bridgetown, or Nusawattocks, the upper county seat. Court was held alternately at these two places.

A man by the name of Walter Williams lived in Bridgetown at this time. He owned a large ordinary, or hotel, the foundations of which still remain. Since there was no courthouse at Bridgetown, Court was held in this ordinary. Walter Williams was licensed March 23, 1646 to keep an ordinary and feeding house, and "to sell strong water." In 1649 the first court was held there and at these very sessions fighting and disorder was mentioned. An example of the kind of cases held there is as follows: For being drunk, Robert Warder was ordered to stand at the Church door at Bridgetown with a great pot tied around his neck.

At this time there was a group of Quakers at Bridgetown, who carried on meetings, at first in the homes of private citizens, and later in a building of their own.

These Quakers were led by William Robinson, who landed them at Bridgetown. Here they were received by Levin Denwood who provided a ten foot log cabin for a house of worship. This was probably the first Quaker meetinghouse in Virginia. After the Act of Toleration passed in 16__, George Brickhouse, a resident of Bridgetown left to the Quaker sect an acre of land surrounding their meetinghouse, and Mrs. Judith Patrick gave them thirty shillings for the repair of the building.

Formerly, there had not been a bridge over the creek at Bridgetown. The travelers had to go four or five miles out of their way, and if they did try to cross, they were endangering their health and lives in doing so. A citizen of this community, William Greening, made a complaint, and on September 20, 1653, a court order to build a bridge over the creek at Nusawattocks was made. Included also in the order was that inhabitants of the whole county should be Contributors to the expense of the bridge. After the completion of the bridge the name of the town was suitably changed from Nusawattocks to Bridgetown.

Since population was increasing and its center was gradually advancing northward, some of the settlers requested the County Court to have a vote taken for the purpose of "making a choice where Ye Courthouse should be for their greatest convenience." It was decided to vote on whether the new courthouse should be held at Bridgetown or "The Horns." "The Horns" which is now called Eastville was equal distance between Bridgetown and "Old Plantation", where the court had been held prior to the time. "The Horns" was selected as the site for the building by one vote and the following order was made by the Court on January 1, 1677. "Whereas by ye votes of ye inhabitants of ye Count of Northampton they have made choice of Henry Mathews his house as ye place called ye Horns for Court doth therefore upon ye petition of ye said Mathews license him to keep an Ordinary there, he entering into bond with sufficient security to perform ye law in such cases provided." "The Horns" later became known as Peachburg and after the first courthouse was erected in 1688, the name was changed to Eastville.

Bridgetown was a rather large industrial center in those days. At Hungar's Wharf, which is right in Bridgetown, large boats and steamers used to come up and trade with the Indians and also engage in slave trade. Then later when the community was more densely populated, the people, who were chiefly farmers, used to send their farm produce to Baltimore, Md. on vessels which left Hungar's Wharf, and moved up to Chesapeake Bay to Baltimore.

Bridgetown was also included in the old stage route. There were two distinct stages on the Peninsula - one from Horntown southbound at 6:30 in the morning, and another northbound from Eastville at the same hour. The coach leaving from Horntown would go through several towns in Accomac, the last one in Accomac being Belle Haven, and then it would continue through Franktown and Bridgetown to the terminus at Eastville. The stage coach was a rather crude affair; it consisted of one horse and a two-wheel cart. It changed horses every twenty miles; Bridgetown was one of the stations where the changes were made.

Some of the historical and interesting buildings around and near Bridgetown are Hungar's Church, the Glebe, Vaucluse, Pear Plain, Chatham, Winona, and Cedar Grove.

Hungar's Church is almost in Bridgetown. This church is one of the oldest churches in the state of Virginia. It is very beautiful and historic looking building - surrounded and hidden by a body of sweet-scented pine and Sycamore trees. The church has four large round arched windows, and two round arched doors in the west front with a smaller window above. Another thing that makes the church so pretty is the ivy which grows all over one of its sides.

In 1642, by the Act of the General Assembly, Northampton County was divided into parishes. "All the land below King's Creek to Smith's Island being one parish, afterwards called Hungar's Parish, and all from King's Creek to Nusawattocks Creek being called Nusawattocks Church or Parish." But at a Council held at James City April 21, 1691, the parishes, Hungars and Nusawattocks were merged into Hungar's Parish. Very soon after this division was made, plans were also made for the building of a church for the parish. In 1684, Major William Spencer gave to the church wardens the land on Hungar's Creek, on which the frame of a church already stood and one acre of land surrounding it. This land given by Major Spencer was part of land grant 600 acres on which Chatham was later built. The church was built soon after 1691. Some of the furnishings put in the church were gifts from Queen Anne of England. In 1741, John Custis of Williamsburg and Arlington presented to Hungar's Church a communion set, but this set is now used in Christ's Church at Eastville.

In 1751, since the old church was somewhat dilapidated, a new church, the one which is there now, was built. Mr. Thomas Preeson, who had been a member of the old church, contributed a sum of money to the building of the new church, on the consideration that he might have a pew in the church marked T.P. The linens and other furnishings given by Queen Anne were transferred from the old church to the new one, but soon they began to become old and worn out, so they were taken to the courthouse in Eastville to be preserved. Services were held in the church until 1840 when it had to be repaired. At this time the building was also slightly reduced in size. Hungars is said to have contained the first pipe organ ever used in America. During the Revolutionary War, when royal things were in disfavor, the metal of this pipe organ was melted and used as sinkers for fish nets. Today Hungar's Church still stands alone and serene in its solemnity and colonial splendor.

A mile west of Hungar's Church is the Glebe farm. In 1653 Colonel Stephen Charlton left this homeplace now known as "The Glebe" in Church Neck to his daughter with the provision that if she had no child the land would go to the church wardens and the vestry of Hungar's Parish for the support of the rector. Since the daughter had no child at her death the parish inherited it. "The Glebe" therefore became the home of many successive rectors. Somehow or other, part of the main Hungar's Church was separated and moved down to the Glebe farm. The Glebe was church property until 1849. Two miles west of the Glebe is Vaucluse, birthplace of Abel Parker Upshur, Secretary of State, who was killed in the explosion on the Princeton in 1844. The present house was built about 1739 by Littleton Upshur, Sr., the father of Abel Upshur. Vaucluse is a lovely old building with identifiable charm and beauty. Adjoining Vaucluse is Pear Plain the home of Colonel Littleton Upshur, an elder son of the judge.

Just outside of Bridgetown, Chatham is located. Chatham was known as Hungar's Plantation until General Pitts bought it in 1618 and changed the name, calling it Chatham for William Pitts, First Early of Chatham. The house at Chatham was built in 1820 by General M.S. Pitts. It is noted for its new interior and its picturesque location.

About a mile from Chatham is Winona. Winona was built by John Severn in 1645. It is possibly the oldest brick building in America. It is a very quaint house with a rare set of Jacobean grouped chimneys.

Cedar Grove, on Hungar's Creek, is another very old farm, located a mile from Bridgetown. The house was built in 1736 by Abel P. Upshur, grandfather of Abel P. Upshur who was Secretary of State and lateral Secretary of the Navy under President Tyler. At Cedar Grove, there is an old grave - that of Ann Emerson Upshur, dated 1775. Cedar Grove also has a lovely lawn with fine cedars and handsome box wood.

One can readily see that Bridgetown and the community around it has played a very important part in the history of the Eastern Shore of Virginia.

1938

― ―

PRIZE WINNER - Miss Dorothy Robbins, daughter of Mr. and Mrs. Bryan Robbins, of Johnsontown, winner of the Old Home Prize (reprinted herewith), at Franktown-Nassawadox High School, session of 1937-1938. Miss Robbins, who was of course Valedictorian of the Senior Class, had the highest four-year average of any class member, having maintained an average of 97 throughout her High School course.

The Bridge of Bridgetown

"Bridgetown—It got its name from the bridge. We have heard and read that it is at the mouth of the creek. What we've been doing is trying to find out where the bridge was. We have reason to believe that there might have been 2 bridges, one of them was where the causeway is now. We asked everybody we visited where the original (1600's) bridge was and no one knows for certain." - Elan Hess

One of the few pictures of what the wooden bridge looked like is found on a postcard. The stamp dates it to 1918. Where was the photo taken? How has the road changed? Which direction is the carriage going? Perhaps it's a stock photo and not of Bridgetown at all. What do you think?

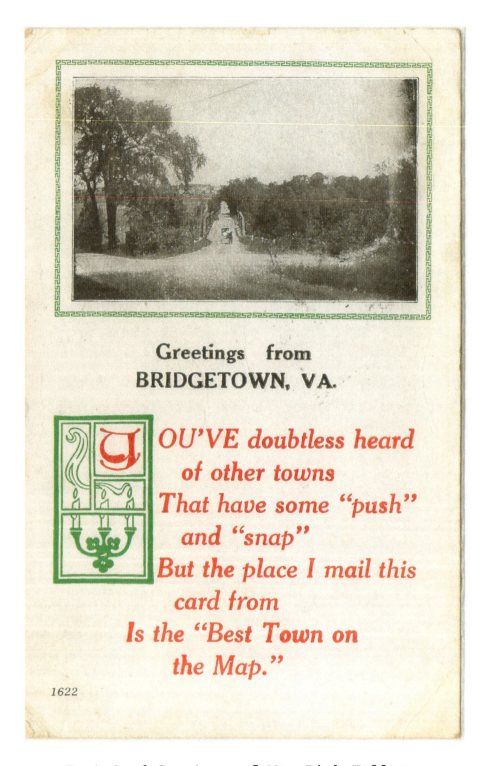

Post Card Courtesy of Mr. Rick Kellam

Dear ___k : -

Am sending your checks today. Keep a look out for them.

    Hastily, Lila...Love to all

It's hard to tell what the first name is. The last letter looks like a k compared to the rest of the writing.

Send Me
Lena's Address

Mrs. Josiah Jolliff
49 St. and Kenova Ave.
Norfolk, VA

On a photo expedition to recreate the angle of the picture on the postcard, an interesting purple sphere appeared in the photos... perhaps to help indicate the location of the original bridge!

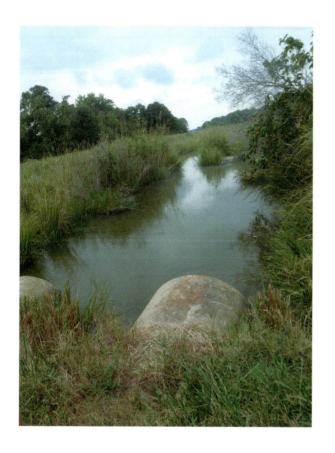

This culvert is all that remains of a bridge at Bridgetown. We don't know exactly when the road was first paved and the pipes put in. Fred Floyd said that in 1926 there was no bridge, just a dirt causeway. As he recalls, back in 1934, the only hard surface road in Northampton County was Route 13. The pipes in the culverts allow the tidal waters of Hungars Creek to flow under Bayside Road.

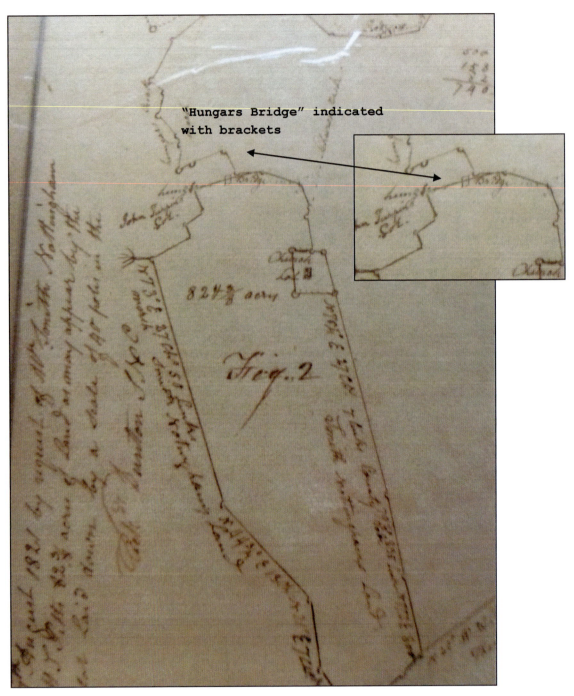

Plat Book #2, p. 41 shows the 1821 survey conducted for Gen. Pitts and indicates Hungars Bridge (see inset).

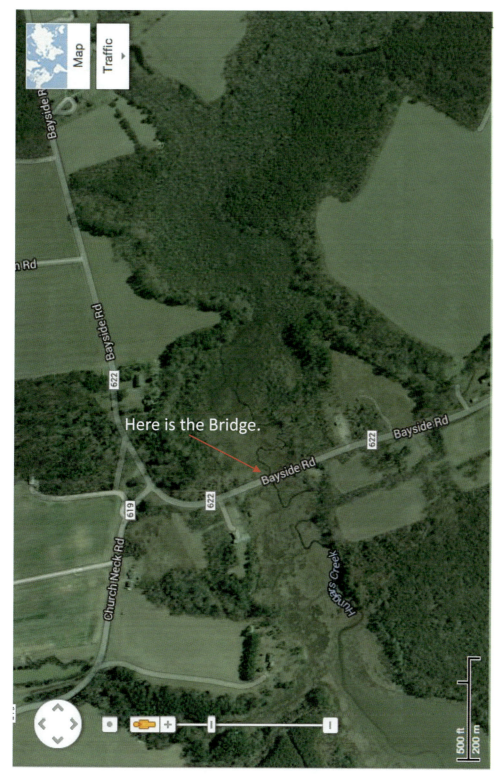

Aerial Map of the Bridgetown area circa 2014. Courtesy Google Maps.

Bridgetown in the E.S. News

Over the years there have been articles in the Eastern Shore News highlighting the history and people of Bridgetown. Our thanks to the Eastern Shore News for letting us reprint three of them here and to Mr. Miles Barnes for his help at the microfiche machine!

chronicles

Our oldest town?

by kirk mariner

What is the oldest town on the Eastern Shore of Virginia?

Accomac—old, but not the oldest—illustrates how difficult it is to answer that seemingly simple question. Accomac was settled for over a century before it became a "town." And to determine which is the oldest town on the peninsula means first to decide when a settlement has grown large enough to be called a "town."

John Dye was the first settler in the place we know as Accomac, back in 1664. His house stood diagonally across the street from today's courthouse, and it later became an "ordinary," or tavern. The county court began convening in the tavern in 1677, but though this was, therefore, the county seat there was no town to speak of, just this one house. Not until 1786 was the Town of Drummond created around the old ordinary. So Drummondtown the town, which was renamed Accomac in 1893, did not come into being until more than a century after the first inhabitant settled there.

Like Accomac, a number of Eastern Shore communities can claim that someone has lived there continuously since the 1600s: Bridgetown, Eastville, Guilford, Assawoman, Onancock, Pungoteague, Chincoteague, Tangier, and Saxis. But in most of these places, and particularly in the islands, it took a number of years for a village to come into being. As "towns," these places cannot necessarily be said to date from the 1600s.

In all of Virginia, and not just the Eastern Shore, towns and villages were a rarity throughout the seventeenth century. The geography of Virginia, the land's "extraordinary accessibility to seaborne traffic," made towns almost unnecessary. For all practical purposes, each of the many isolated plantations was a self-contained little village. And far more desirable than gathering into communities was owning one's own plantation and shipping one's own crop of tobacco from one's own private wharf. Among the many people who lamented the absence of towns in early Virginia was the Presbyterian minister Francis Makemie, who in 1705 published **A Plain and Friendly Perswasive to the Inhabitants of Virginia and Maryland, for Promoting Towns and Cohabitation**. Yet despite the advice of Makemie and many others, most Virginians could simply not be entied to live in towns.

The first town on the Eastern Shore of Virginia was one that no longer exists: "The Towne," established in the 1620s on King's Creek west of Cheriton. Here surrounded by a stockade was a regular little village: church, courthouse, warehouses, wharves, residences. But the Eastern Shore was then frontier, and the Towne a fort-like place to guarantee the security of the few settlers. As the population of the Shore grew, few chose to live in the Towne; most preferred to carve out their own plantation.

The Towne was abandoned in 1677, and by then another village had come into being further up the peninsula. This second village is today the oldest continuously inhabited community on the Eastern Shore of Virginia: Bridgetown. Unlike the Towne, Bridgetown was not planned or built from scratch; it simply grew up gradually around the spot where the main road of the peninsula crossed Hungars Creek. In 1677 when a new place known to us as Eastville was chosen as the site for the county court, Bridgetown was already a recognizable village. Eastville, by comparison, was a single house, "where Henry Matthews now liveth."

Scholars agree that Bridgetown is the oldest town on the Shore, but disagree about which town is second. According to some it is Pungoteague. By 1677 Pungoteague was the site of a church—but did the church follow the emergence of a village there, or did a village emerge because a church was built there?

Onancock is, at the very least, the third oldest town on the Shore, after Bridgetown and possibly Pungoteague. Christopher Calvert settled in what became Onancock in 1655, like John Dye in Accomac the first and only inhabitant. The town came into being a quarter century later in 1680, when the legislature in Jamestown, recognizing the need for settled towns and villages, passed an "Act of Cohabitation" which was designed to establish a port town in each county. In 1681 Daniel Jenifer laid out the streets in the new port town of Accomack County, taking care to incorporate Calvert's place, which was already there, in his design. In the early years Onancock was known as Scarburgh or Port Scarburgh, and it can justly claim, as surprisingly few places in Virginia can, to be over three hundred years old.

Though some of our towns date from the 1600s, few if any of them can boast a single landmark dating from that early century. The churches, houses, buildings, even the roads that comprised those early villages have long since disappeared.

Onancock is the notable exception. In Onancock you can stroll back into the 1600s because the streets in the oldest part of town still follow the pattern laid down in 1681. North Street was then the eastern boundary of town. It and Market Street and King Street were right there in the seventeenth century, and that little square next to Cokesbury Church has been there since the days when Francis Makemie lived just down the street. This old street pattern is the only landmark from the 1600s still visible in any town on the Eastern Shore of Virginia today.

And when these streets were created, the village of Bridgetown was already in existence. Onancock notwithstanding, Bridgetown is our oldest town.

Copyright 1985 by Kirk Mariner

Printed in the Eastern Shore News March 15, 1985
Reprinted here courtesy of Mr. Kirk Mariner

WEDNESDAY, MAY 5, 1999

It was one of the Shore's busy places

ON THE SALTY SIDE

RANDOLPH WALKER

It only takes about 15 seconds to ride through it now, but it is reputed to be the oldest continuously inhabited village on the Eastern Shore. We're talking about Bridgetown, in Northampton County. It was settled sometime in the early 17th century and had a long and active life until a few years ago.

Coming down Route 13, turn off on Bayside Rd. at Exmore and go about eight miles until you get to Hungar's Episcopal Church. Now you're in Bridgetown. But all that's left from this once busy little place now is the church, two of three houses left with inhabitants, a couple of buildings in ruins, ready to collapse, and Shorter's Chapel. There is only one inhabited house left in downtown Bridgetown.

On Sunday mornings communicants of Hungar's and Shorter's Chapel restore some activity to Bridgetown, but on all other days, only the dumpsters attract traffic.

The bridge from which the settlement took its name is now a road across a marsh which once was a deep spacious creek. In its early days the location was a port for schooners and smaller craft that sailed up Hungar's Creek and moored to pine trees lining the creek bank. Now, a half mile or so inside Hungar's Creek from the Bay, the creek is very shallow and allows access to only small outboards and such. Three hundred years of cutting timber along the banks along with heavy farming has filled the once deep creek.

Ghosts of the past lurk on both sides of the road in Bridgetown as autos speed by. Local residents can remember several businesses that supplied the surrounding area, and they included the Hastings general store, the Floyd general store, an eatery described as one that served fried fish sandwiches, a pool hall and dance establishment, and one or two houses that have long since sunk into the marsh.

Reprinted from the Eastern Shore News May 5, 1999

The Hastings store was located approximately where county dumpsters are now. The post office, established in 1835, was situated in the store. Later, Hastings built a small building next to his store to house the post office. The Floyd store was across the road from Hastings, on a site now obscured by marsh.

Bear in mind that Bridgetown was on the main road down the Shore in those days and all Shore traffic passed through this busy town. It also was a port where farmers located produce to be shipped to the cities. Boats, some with three masts, moved cotton, wheat and vegetables in and out of Bridgetown on a regular basis.

County court was held in Bridgetown in the early days as it was in Eastville. Early on, citizens of the county had to decide which town would be the county seat. Citizens decided by one vote that it would be Eastville.

When the railroad was laid down the Shore in 1884, one of the stops was Bridgetown station, even though the town itself was a couple of miles from the track. Hey, this was quite a place! This busy hub of commerce was served by water, highway and the railroad. Later the railroad changed the name of its station to Birdsnest.

I'd like to have seen Bridgetown in its heyday on that deep, wide creek when the sounds of creaking masts, squeaking wagon wheels, and the hum of many voices sounded as the commerce of the Shore played out its life in this busy port. Workers shouted to each other as they loaded the boats, wagons rumbled across the wooden bridge on the way back and forth to the railroad station, men and women lounged on the porches of the restaurants, and later, the sound of music came from the pool hall as children played alongside the road.

Bridgetown was a glimpse of life on the Eastern Shore as it was in the centuries past.

Note: The dumpsters were removed when the service center at Birdsnest was opened.

PORTRAIT

An Individual Profile

by James Kennedy

RICHARD S. FLOYD, JR.
Church Neck, Va.

He Bought His First Cow When He Was Twelve. Owned His Own Grocery Store Before He Was Twenty. At 77, This Enterprising Shoreman Still Farms, Buys And Sells Produce...Races Horses On The Side.

Richard S. Floyd, Jr. and his wife today live on "Pear Plain" farm in a lovely old house, the original part of which was built in the early part of the last century. Mr. Floyd was born July 27, 1897 on this same farmland in another house which no longer stands today.

The farm was named Pear Plain because it once had a large pear orchard on it. Another fact of historical interest is that the first Hungars Church was on the Pear Plain land 150 or more years ago.

Ever since he was a boy, Richard Floyd had wanted to own the house and land where he lives today. And in 1932 he was able to realize that childhood ambition. They have lived there happily ever since.

Young Richard got his first schooling in a one-room school house that was also located on the Pear Plain farmland. "All the kids living on Church Neck went there," he said. And he recalled that Mrs. Walker Ames was his first teacher.

Richard was a rather important pupil. "I drove the school bus," he said. He was only 12 years old at the time. And actually it wasn't a 'bus' at all but a farm wagon drawn by a team of two horses. Mr. Floyd learned how to handle farm animals at a very early age.

He next went to school at Bridgetown Academy. This building still stands today but it is now a residence. He was a catcher on the Academy baseball team, and played a little football. But he gave up this body-contact sport when he got tackled one day by a much bigger fellow. "I got rolled down the hill," he recalled.

After graduating from Bridgetown Academy, he went to Beacom Business College in Salisbury for one year, then returned to help out in his father's grocery store in nearby Johnson. It was a typical general store of that era, selling just about everything. "We sold plough points, horse collars and toothpicks." The shelves were well stocked with shoes and clothes for men and women. Farm families could find just about everything they needed at Floyd's General Store.

He recalled that flour, coffee, corn meal and many other grocery items were then sold in bulk. Canned goods were just beginning to appear on grocery shelves. There were no frozen foods, of course. And fresh vegetables were available at the store only when local farmers harvested their crops. Perishable foods were not then shipped from distant southern states during wintertime. The luxury of a year-round enjoyment of green vegetables which all of us take for granted today was not then known.

When he was not quite 20 years old, Richard Floyd became the proud owner of his own grocery store. He bought out William Wilkins' interest in the Bridgetown store that he and Frank Spady had operated. Mr. Floyd lost this first store in a disastrous fire. But undaunted, he built another store to replace it. He survived a few robberies. Yes, they had break-ins even in those days. And one time, he recalled, the thieves carted off his safe.

But despite adversities, his grocery business flourished. And now he began to specialize in meats. He built his own slaughterhouse, killing cows, hogs and lambs that he raised himself. At first he did this just to supply his own local customers. But after a while he delivered fresh meats to stores located as far south as Cape Charles and north to Onley. In time he built up a big business up and down the Shore in sausage meat and hamburger back in the pre-inflation days when those two popular meat-products sold for around 39¢ a pound, believe it or not.

Mr. Floyd was always enterprising. In addition to running a grocery store and operating his own wholesale meat business, he also did a lot of traveling when he was a young man.

Before tractors came into general use on Eastern Shore farms, there was a big demand here for farm horses and mules. Mr. Floyd became one of the leading suppliers of these farm animals. He went to horse and mule auctions all over the country. He attended many sales in Johnson City, Tennessee, the Grand Island auctions in Nebraska near Omaha. He traveled as far west as Montana in search of farm animals to supply a demand that then existed on the Eastern Shore.

Mr. Floyd is basically a farmer. But for most of his life he has always been involved in the buying and selling of produce and farm animals. He bought his first cow when he was only twelve years old. He bought many more since then. Today he still operates his own grading shed each year; still farms from 200 to 300 acres, mostly planted in potatoes. And he still owns a small stable of race-horses. His father owned race-horses, and Richard Floyd, Jr. has owned pacers and trotters ever since he was about 20 years old.

So, this life-long interest in harness-racing horses was something he came by quite naturally. Even as a boy, he remembers watching race-horses that his father owned at the old Keller Fair Grounds and other nearby harness tracks. Horse-racing is one of the oldest of sports. It's something that "gets in the blood".

Following in his Dad's footsteps, Mr. Floyd has owned quite a few harness-track winners. He mentioned particularly Blue Field, Sultan Hanover, June 1st and Shady Dale. Each of these thoroughbreds won purses totaling around $90,000 when they raced under Mr. Floyd's ownership.

In earlier years he raced his horses at some of the largest harness tracks in the East. Such as Yonkers Raceway and Wesbury around New York. He still sends horses to the post almost every year at Rosecroft near Washington, D. C., Dover Downs, Harrington and Brandywine in Delaware and Ocean Downs in Maryland.

He still owns about seven trotters and pacers which he keeps in training at his own practice track in Birds Nest. His brother, Louis H. Floyd, is the trainer and driver for this jointly owned stable. Richard has never been a driver, himself. But his brother, Louis, now 62, will again be found in the seat of a sulky as a row of spirited pacers or trotters line up behind the starting gate at Ocean Downs this summer.

And whenever the Floyd brothers have a horse entered in a race with a chance to capture the winner's purse, it's a safe assumption that Richard, age 77, will be at the trackside either physically or "in spirit", rooting their horse home. It is probably Richard Floyd's continuing interest in the sport of racing that keeps him looking so young.

Mr. Floyd has two other hobbies that keep him occupied. One of these is an outdoor sport -- rabbit-hunting. He has always owned and trained rabbit dogs. The other is an indoor pastime that he shares with his wife. It's a card game that they call "Set Back". In the winter they match their wits and card-playing skills with their friends and neighbors. They don't play for money -- just for fun.

Eastern Shore News March 28, 1974

Bridgetown Post Office

> "So if you live in Bridgetown, why is your address Machipongo?"

The Bridgetown Post Office, zip code 23309, closed in 1967 after 128 years of service. Mrs. Lillian S. Ames served for 32 1/2 years as the last postmistress.

When the Bridgetown Post Office closed, mail delivery was switched to the Machipongo Post Office, zip code 23405.

William T. Hastings at the Bridgetown Post Office circa 1950

Photo courtesy of Jenny Floyd

GENERAL SERVICES ADMINISTRATION

National Archives and Records Service
Washington 25, D. C.

March 7, 1951
(April 20, 1951 COPIES)

C O P Y

Miss Lillian S. Ames, Postmaster
Bridgetown, Virginia

My dear Miss Ames:

This is in reply to your letter of Feburary 7, 1951 to the National Archives regarding the post office at Bridgetown, Northampton County, Virginia.

Records of the Post Office Department now in the National Archives do not contain any references to a post office at Bridgetown, Virginia, earlier than 1839. A post office was established there on August 17, 1839, its name was changed to Johnstown on May 10, 1843, and back to Bridgetown on December 8, 1875. It was discontinued on July 31, 1920 and reestablished on May 7, 1921. Names of postmasters and dates of their appointment to 1930 were:

Postmaster	Date of Appointment
Benjamin Betate *Belote*	August 17, 1839
Rufus Heath	December 23, 1841
Thomas B. Williams	April 13, 1842
John E. Taylor *Leathebury*	August 16, 1842
William I. Seatherburg	May 10, 1843
col — Albert G. Holt	February 16, 1855
Victor A. Mapp, Jr.	January 24, 1859
George R. Jacob	February 14, 1866
I. C. Roberts	April 4, 1867
J. R. Mapp	May 8, 1867
Victor A. Mapp, Jr.	October 23, 1867
James A. Jarvis	April 18, 1870
Joseph W. Thomas	November 30, 1875
George R. Mapp	December 8, 1875
col — Alfred T. Trehurn	May 17, 1883
col — Leonard Trehurn	February 28, 1884
Edmund W. Roberts	July 16, 1885
William R. Wilkins	May 16, 1897
Edmund W. Roberts	November 14, 1905
Ruth M. Boss *(madeline)*	June 8, 1916
Hoge Hegs A. Floyd	April 14, 1919
Richard S. Floyd, Jr.	May 7, 1921
Sampson T. Truitt	November 22, 1923
William T. Hastings	September 2, 1927
	(still serving in 1930)

This excerpt from a letter to Mrs. Lillian S. Ames from the office of the Chief Archivist, Industrial Records Branch of the General Service Administration details the history of the Bridgetown Post Office.

Additional postmasters:
Charles C. Mapp (Acting) October 1, 1934
Mrs. Lillian S. Ames March 6, 1935 until her retirement when the post office closed on Aug. 31, 1967.

Hungars Church

Since the assignment of the first minister in 1623, there have been three church buildings known as "Hungars Church." The first of these three was built around 1646 on land acquired through Richard Vaughan's bequest in 1645 of tobacco "toward the building of a house of God's service." This church, known first as "Nusswattocks Church" stood about 150 yards north of Pear Plain on the west bank of Hungars Creek.— Excerpt from www.hungarscureparish.org

The current church is the third building and is a shortened version of the building erected circa 1742. Hungars Church is widely known for its recently added 969-pipe Holtkamp custom built organ.

"I made Hungars Church on Minecraft. What is Minecraft, you ask? Minecraft is a virtual world made out of blocks. We built Bridgetown from the ground up in this virtual world. As you can see in the picture, it is pretty accurate to the real one." - Elan Hess

Stephen S. Gunter: The Reverend Blacksmith

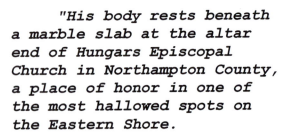

"His body rests beneath a marble slab at the altar end of Hungars Episcopal Church in Northampton County, a place of honor in one of the most hallowed spots on the Eastern Shore.

He is the only rector buried in the venerable churchyard. Yet he was really a blacksmith, and a Methodist."

So begins the tale of Rev. Stephen Gunter as told by Kirk Mariner and Jean M. Mihalyka in "True Tales of the Eastern Shore." It's a fascinating story that is worth reading! See the box on the right for the full inscription on the tomb stone.

> *Sacred to the memory of Rev. Stephen S. Gunter who was born in Accomack County, E. S. of Va. on the 20th of J... 1792. He was chosen rector of Hungars Parish 1823 where he continued until October 1st, 1835 when he was called at the age of 43 years to the rest which remaineth for the people of God. Let me die the death of the righteous and let my last end be like his. This stone was erected by his parishoners as a tribute of their affectionate remembrance.*

Shorter's Chapel

"The Church That Sits On The Hill With Doors That Swing On Friendly Hinges."

According to Reverend Debbie Bryant, Shorter's Chapel was founded in 1866 after the Civil War. A.M.E stands for African Methodist Episcopal. Missionaries came to Bridgetown to teach the slaves and there were two schools for slaves here. Rev. Bryant is a member of the Historic Bridgetown Association, that would like to see an historic marker erected to honor Bridgetown's heritage.

Sam's Corner

"Some people saw Sam as a friend, others as family, and the rest of us as the sign at Sam's Corner. The people who knew Sam told stories about him, and the people who just saw the sign listened. Sam wasn't wealthy, not many on the Shore were. He lived in a trailer and only had a hot plate to cook on. Sam was a friend to us all, even the ones who didn't know him. Next time you are in Bridgetown look for the Sam's Corner sign." - Forest Flynn

"Let's meet at Sam's Corner!"

Reid H. Diggs III made this sign that hangs at the corner of Church Neck Road and Bayside Road. Reid said that when he was young everyone used Sam's Hill or Sam's Corner as a local landmark. The sign was his way of paying tribute to Sam Trower whose store, and later trailer, stood on that corner.

Chatham

Today the majority of tourists to the Bridgetown area are on their way to Chatham Vineyards. The Church Creek label is known throughout the country for their award-winning wines. Chatham has been a working farm for four centuries and the brick house dates to 1818. The vineyards are owned and operated by the Wehner Family. The Kayak Winery Tour is an Eastern Shore classic!

The vineyard at the end of the Rainbow!

~ Winona ~
A tale of three chimneys

"Winona was my favorite place of all of them. When we walked in Mrs. Walker had Chocolate Chip cookies baking. The house was really cool to tour. But my favorite part was the chimneys. They had three chimneys but not separate. They were all together you'll have to look at the picture of the chimneys for yourself." - Forest Flynn

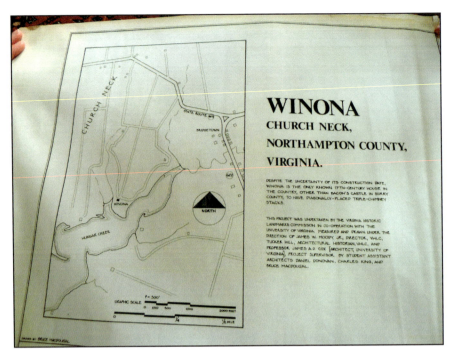

"*Winona is the only known 17th-century house in the country, other than Bacon's Castle in Surry County, to have diagonally-placed triple-chimney stacks.*"
- Winona Historical Architectural Project

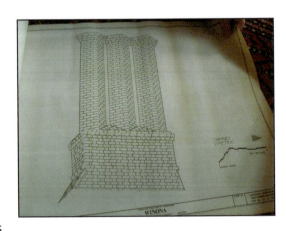

"Even though Whitelaw gives Winona a seventeenth century date, there is no concrete evidence to support that, and we have never found the dated brick to which he refers. Our broad guess is that it was built in the early 18th century, at least by 1750. Hills Farm in Accomac Co., similar in design to the Glebe, was dated to 1747 by dendrochronology. Winona is quite primitive in design and interior detailing when compared to either of these two houses, so possibly was built a bit earlier, but who knows?! (Maybe our children will get the testing done on the beams in the cellar one day and the truth will come out.) The Jacobean chimneys are notable and possibly led Whitelaw to the early date. We have no idea why this architectural holdover from the previous century was brought back to life at Winona.

Herman and I moved to Winona in June of 1968. The house had been rented and stood vacant off and on for fifteen years and was in rough shape. The west wing was added at that same time, and we did a little fixing up to the old house including a total re-do of the 1895 kitchen (which had been put on when the house was purchased by Herman's great-grandfather, Laban Belote). We added the sunroom on the east in 2005 and since then have been able to enjoy the great view of Hungars Creek where it is said that sailing ships came in to Winona's dock to pick up the harvested potatoes." - Mary Walker 2014

Mary Walker's Chocolate Chip Cookies

Set oven to 350 degrees

1 cup butter, softened (your fat needs answered for a week!)

1/2 cup sugar

1 cup brown sugar

2 eggs, room temperature

2 teaspoons vanilla extract

2 3/4 flour (I used 1 cup garbanzo bean flour from Quail Cove and 3/4 cup fine oatmeal with 1 cup reg. flour) (You could use all regular flour.)

1 1/2 teaspoon baking powder

2 1/4 cups semi-sweet chocolate drops

Cream butter and sugars with a mixer for 3 minutes; add eggs and vanilla and beat for 2 minutes; mix dry ingredients together and fold into the butter mixture, add chocolate bits, stir together lightly, and put on cookie sheet with ice cream scoop or tablespoon. Bake for 12-14 minutes until brown around the edges. Enjoy!

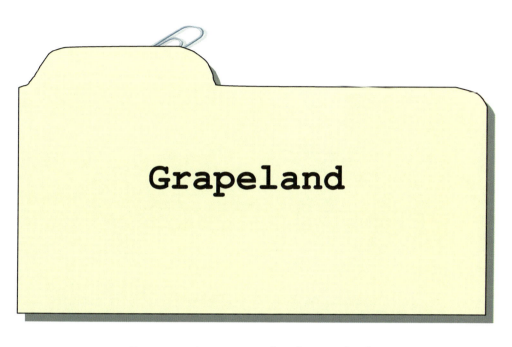

Grapeland

Report on Visit with

Mr. Philip Bernard Tankard 9/30/13

"Grapeland was built in 1642. A beam in the basement was a ship mast. There is a cemetery at Grapeland. Grapeland was built to take advantage of the breeze. There is water at Grapeland so ships could dock and take off."

- Liam Flynn, age 9

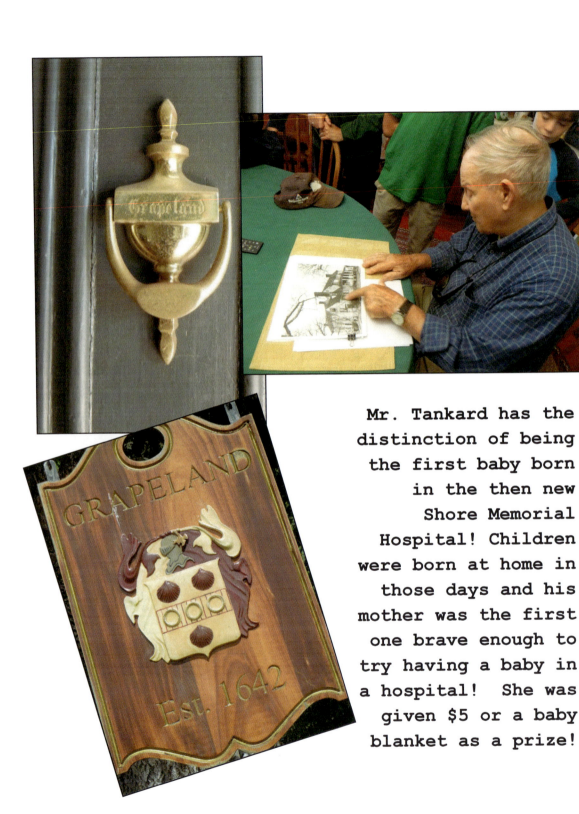

Mr. Tankard has the distinction of being the first baby born in the then new Shore Memorial Hospital! Children were born at home in those days and his mother was the first one brave enough to try having a baby in a hospital! She was given $5 or a baby blanket as a prize!

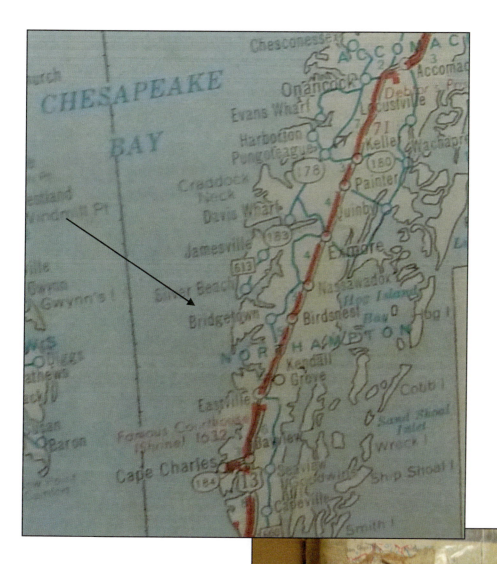

Bridgetown could be seen on the cover of the Rand McNally Atlas circa 1950. Shown here courtesy of Mr. Philip B. Tankard.

G. Fred Floyd Jr.

"Fred" Floyd at 87 has lived the longest time in Bridgetown. He moved to his farm when he was two years old. He can tell all sorts of stories about Bridgetown. His daughter, Jenny Floyd, was an incredible help with the "Bridgetown Files" project. She created maps, shared the photos of the old stores, and made connections with knowledgeable people. The Floyd family's history and genealogy is a big part of connecting the past with present day Bridgetown.

Photos of Bridgetown Stores
courtesy of Jenny and Fred Floyd

```
Top left:Original W.T. Hastings Store Pre-1930
Top right: W.T.Hastings New Store circa 1930
Bottom left: R.S. Floyd Store circa 1965
Bottom right: Bridgetown as it was.
```

Pear Plain

"N72A Because they are within a few feet of each other, this site symbol is used for four sites: a house, an unusual tree, a court tavern, and an old church." - from "Virginia's Eastern Shore" by Ralph Whitelaw

Whitelaw goes on to describe the house, the huge hackberry tree which is no longer standing, the tavern (or ordinary) where court was held in the 1600's, and the original site of Hungars Church. He concludes the history of site N72A with this reference and comment:

"1694 An entry refers to 'Hungars old Church Neck,' and down to the present time the whole neck is called Church Neck."

Historian Jenean Hall explaining her theories of where the 1600's original bridges might have been in relation to Pear Plain.

Google maps still show "Paraplane Cove." Is this where Pear Plain got its name, not from fruit?

Jane Turner, whose family lives at Pear Plain, and Jenean Hall discuss genealogy...and discover they're related!

Fun Facts

- Did you know that Northampton County has the oldest continuous court records in the United States, dating to 1632? You can go to the county clerk's office and look at them anytime and do your own research!

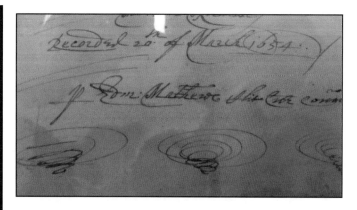

This court record reads "Recorded 20th of March 1654" which would be 1655 if New Year's was January 1st instead of March 25th. The cool spirals are doodles that appear quite often in the records.

- A word on dates: Until about 1753, the English celebrated New Year's Day on March 25th. That means when you look at the old records, December 31, 1649 would be followed by January 1, 1649 and March 24, 1649 would be followed by March 25, 1650. So when you read the court records, remember to think about the dates for the months of January, February and March as being recorded as what we would perceive as the previous year. Historian Jenean Hall solves this problem by writing double dates for those months, for example March 20, 1654/55.

- Some people say that Bridgetown was known as a "rough and tumble" town! They even recall stories of a circus coming to town with a black bear that people could wrestle!

The Bear Wins!!

Sandi Johnson and Jean Flynn

- Forest Flynn's family on his mother's side (Jean Johnson Flynn) are direct descendants of Capt. William Eppes. Whitelaw's shows Capt. Eppes as coming to the Eastern Shore in 1621 and he owned land next to Tom Savage. The family didn't know this until long after they moved to the Eastern Shore. Now, thanks to the research of genealogist and historian, Sandi Johnson (Forest's grandmother), they discovered they are "come back here's!"

- Native Americans lived on the Eastern Shore for thousands of years before the colonists arrived. Artifacts such as stone tools and projectile points can be found in the fields and marshes. Church Neck residents, Bob Bredimus and Jane Turner, each have very impressive collections of items found locally. As this book goes to press in the Spring of 2014, an archaeological dig near the Glebe was looking for remnants of a Native American settlement. What will they find??

Left to right: Northampton County Clerk Traci Johnson at archaeological dig May 2014. Projectile points from the collection of Mr. Bob Bredimus on display at the Barrier Islands Center. VA State Archaeologist Dr. Mike Barber.

THE ANIMALS OF BRIDGETOWN

SHEEP!!! Jen and Robert Bridges (Yes, the Bridges of Bridgetown!) have a flock of four rare Hog Island Sheep. This is a heritage breed of sheep that came directly off the island.

HORSES!!! There is a long history of horses at Bridgetown. Jenean Hall tells the story of a horse race in 1672 by the two Starkye brothers which ends with the accidental death of Nathaniel. The Floyd family owned race horses and there was a race track nearby in the mid-1900's. Today, many people come to Bridgetown for the annual invitational Trail Rides that cover miles of scenic trails.

THINK GLOBALLY AND GROW LOCALLY!!!
True to our rural heritage, you will find Bridgetown today is full of people living close to the land. Neighbors grow their own food and raise chickens, guinea hens, bees, goats, horses, cats, dogs, and even alpacas!

NEW WORLD AND OLD WORLD COMPARISON

On July 17, 1717, there is an entry in the court records that gives very detailed instructions on how to re-build the bridge that has been in disrepair. The court allows 1,000 pounds of tobacco towards the bridge to be made of pine "sleepers" and dimensions such that "the said bridge to be ten foot wide at least with framed rails on each side three foot above the bridge of some durable wood ye said bridge to be so laid that it may be overflowed at High Water, all to be done firm and substantial workmanlike, ye said District to take care and keep ye same in repair…." Quote courtesy of Jenean Hall from Mackey, Vol. 16, p. 24

And what was happening on this date in England? It so happens that on July 17, 1717 a very different crossing of water was in the news. King George I was floating down the Thames on the royal barge, while the composer George Frideric Handel floated on a second barge with fifty musicians deputing the famous "Water Music" orchestral suites. Old World pomp and circumstance compared to New World sustainable bridge building!

That's the story of Bridgetown!

A WORD OF THANKS

We are grateful to all the people who helped us with this project, especially those we have mentioned throughout this book. Additional thanks go to Elvin Hess, Jean and Terry Flynn, Liam Flynn, Jerry Doughty, Laura Vaughan and the staff at the Barrier Islands Center, Tristan Mariner, the County Clerk's office, and all the people of Bridgetown past, present and future. Thanks for exploring the mystery of history with us!

RECOMMENDED READING

"Virginia's Eastern Shore" by Ralph T. Whitelaw

"True Tales of the Eastern Shore" by Kirk Mariner

"Off 13: The Eastern Shore of Virginia Guidebook" by Kirk Mariner

The forthcoming book by Jenean Hall (title to be decided)

"Life for Me Ain't Been No Crystal Stair" by Francis B. Latimer

"The Eastern Shore of Virginia in Days Past" by Julie V. Nordstrom

"Eastern Shore of Virginia, 1603-1964" by Nora Miller Turman

About the Authors...
... History Detectives

Forest Flynn is a 13-year old homeschooler. He was born and raised in Bridgetown. He enjoys playing the guitar, theater, and sports.

Elan Hess is a 12-year old homeschooler. He moved to Bridgetown with his family in 2011. He enjoys karate, building with Legos, and nature.

Annie Hess lives in Bridgetown with her husband, Elvin. She enjoys the bounty of the land and community.

The three authors agree that creating this home school project was AWESOME!

Made in the USA
Charleston, SC
16 December 2014